The Ki

Sorceress of Endor

*

The Truth About Necromancy

Ellen G. White

CONTENTS

THE WITCH OF ENDOR & THE DEATH OF SAUL

—Again, war was declared between Israel and the Philistines. "The Philistines gathered themselves together, and came and pitched in Shunem," on the northern edge of the plain of Jezreel; while Saul and his forces encamped but a few miles distant, at the foot of Mount Gilboa, on the southern border of the plain. It was on this plain that Gideon, with three hundred men, had put to flight the hosts of Midian. But the spirit that inspired Israel's deliverer was widely different from that which now stirred the heart of the king. Gideon went forth strong in faith in the mighty God of Jacob; but Saul felt himself to be alone and defenseless, because God had forsaken him. As he looked abroad upon the Philistine host, "he was afraid, and his heart greatly trembled." Saul had learned that David and his force were with the Philistines, and he expected that the son of Jesse would take this opportunity to revenge the wrongs he had suffered. The king was in sore distress. It was his own unreasoning passion, spurring him on to destroy the chosen of God, that had involved the nation in so great peril. While he had been engrossed in pursuing David he had neglected the defense of his kingdom. The Philistines, taking advantage of its unguarded condition, had penetrated into the very heart of the country. Thus while Satan had been urging Saul to employ every energy in hunting David, that he might destroy him, the same malignant spirit had inspired the Philistines to seize their opportunity to work Saul's ruin and overthrow the people of God. How often is the same policy still employed by the archenemy! He moves upon some unconsecrated heart to kindle envy and strife in the church, and then, taking advantage of the divided condition of God's people, he stirs up his agents to work their ruin. On the morrow Saul must engage the Philistines in battle. The shadows of impending doom gathered dark about him; he longed for help and guidance. But it was in vain that he sought counsel from God. "The Lord answered him not, neither by dreams, nor by Urim, nor by prophets." The Lord never turned away a soul that came to Him in sincerity and humility. Why did he turn Saul away unanswered? The king had by his own act forfeited the benefits of all the methods of inquiring of God. He had rejected the counsel of Samuel the prophet; he had exiled David, the chosen of God; he had slain the priests of the Lord. Could he expect to be answered by God when he had cut off the channels of communication that Heaven had ordained? He had sinned away the Spirit of grace, and could he be answered by dreams and revelations from the Lord? Saul did not turn to God with humility and repentance. It was not pardon for sin and reconciliation with God, that he sought, but deliverance from his foes. By his own stubbornness and rebellion he had cut himself off from God. There could be no return but by the way of penitence and contrition; but the proud monarch, in his anguish and despair, determined to seek help from another source. "Then said Saul unto his servants, Seek me a woman that hath a familiar spirit, that I may go to her, and inquire of her." Saul had a full knowledge of the character of necromancy. It had been expressly forbidden by the Lord, and the sentence of death was pronounced against all who practiced its unholy arts.

During the life of Samuel, Saul had commanded that all wizards and those that had familiar spirits should be put to death; but now, in the rashness of desperation, he had recourse to that oracle which he had condemned as an abomination. It was told the king that a woman who had a familiar spirit was living in concealment at Endor. This woman had entered into covenant with Satan to yield herself to his control, to fulfill his purposes; and in return, the prince of evil wrought wonders for her and revealed secret things to her. Disguising himself, Saul went forth by night with but two attendants, to seek the retreat of the sorceress. Oh, pitiable sight! the king of Israel led captive by Satan at his will! What path so dark for human feet to tread as that chosen by one who has persisted in having his own way, resisting the holy influences of the Spirit of God! What bondage so terrible as that of him who is given over to the control of the worst of tyrants—himself! Trust in God and obedience to His will were the only conditions upon which Saul could be king of Israel. Had he complied with these conditions throughout his reign, his kingdom would have been secure; God would have been his guide, the Omnipotent his shield. God had borne long with Saul; and although his rebellion and obstinacy had well-nigh silenced the divine voice in the soul, there was still opportunity for repentance. But when in his peril he turned from God to obtain light from a confederate of Satan, he had cut the last tie that bound him to his Maker; he had placed himself fully under the control of that demoniac power which for years had been exercised upon him, and which had brought him to the verge of destruction. Under the cover of darkness Saul and his attendants made their way across the plain, and, safely passing the Philistine host, they crossed the mountain ridge, to the lonely home of the sorceress of Endor. Here the woman with a familiar spirit had hidden herself away that she might secretly continue her profane incantations. Disguised as he was, Saul's lofty stature and kingly port declared that he was no common soldier. The woman suspected that her visitor was Saul, and his rich gifts strengthened her suspicions. To his request, "I pray thee, divine unto me by the familiar spirit, and bring me him up, whom I shall name unto thee," the woman answered, "Behold, thou knowest what Saul hath done, how he hath cut off those that have familiar spirits, and the wizards, out of the land: wherefore then layest thou a snare for my life, to cause me to die?" Then "Saul sware to her by the Lord, saying, As the Lord liveth, there shall no punishment happen to thee for this thing." And when she said, "Whom shall I bring up unto thee?" he answered, "Samuel." After practicing her incantations, she said, "I saw gods ascending out of the earth.... An old man cometh up; and he is covered with a mantle. And Saul perceived that it was Samuel, and he stooped with his face to the ground, and bowed himself." It was not God's holy prophet that came forth at the spell of a sorcerer's incantation. Samuel was not present in that haunt of evil spirits. That supernatural appearance was produced solely by the power of Satan. He could as easily assume the form of Samuel as he could assume that of an angel of light, when he tempted Christ in the wilderness. The woman's first words under the spell of her incantation had been addressed to the king, "Why hast thou deceived me? for thou art Saul." Thus the first act of the evil spirit which personated the prophet was to communicate secretly with this wicked woman, to warn her of the deception that had been practiced upon her. The message to Saul from the pretended prophet was, "Why hast thou disquieted me, to bring me up? And Saul answered, I am sore distressed; for the Philistines make war against me, and God is departed from me, and answereth me no more, neither by prophets, nor by dreams: therefore I have called thee, that thou mayest make known unto me what I shall do." When Samuel was living, Saul had despised his counsel and had resented his reproofs. But now, in the hour of his distress and calamity, he felt that the prophet's guidance was his only hope, and in order to communicate with Heaven's ambassador he vainly had recourse to the messenger of hell! Saul had placed himself fully in the power of Satan; and now he whose only delight is in causing misery and destruction, made the most of his advantage, to work the ruin of the unhappy king. In answer to Saul's agonized entreaty came the terrible message, professedly from the lips of Samuel: "Wherefore then dost thou ask of me, seeing the Lord is departed from thee, and is become thine enemy? And the Lord hath done to him, as he spake by me: for the Lord hath rent the kingdom out of thine hand, and given it to thy neighbor, even to David: because thou obeyedst not the voice of the Lord, nor executedst His fierce wrath upon Amalek, therefore hath the Lord done this thing unto thee this day. Moreover the Lord will also deliver Israel with thee into the hand of the Philistines." All through his course of rebellion Saul had been flattered and deceived by Satan. It is the tempter's work to belittle sin, to make the path of transgression easy and inviting, to blind the mind to the warnings and threatenings of the Lord. Satan, by his bewitching power, had led Saul to justify himself in defiance of Samuel's reproofs and warning. But now, in his extremity, he turned upon him, presenting the enormity of his sin and the hopelessness of pardon, that he might goad him to desperation. Nothing could have been better chosen to destroy his courage and confuse his judgment, or to drive him to despair and self-destruction. Saul was faint with weariness and fasting; he was terrified and conscience-stricken. As the fearful prediction fell upon his ear, his form swayed like an oak before the tempest, and he fell prostrate to the earth. The sorceress was filled with alarm. The king of Israel lay before her like one dead. Should he perish in her retreat, what would be the consequences to herself? She besought him to arise and partake of food, urging that since she had imperiled her life in granting his desire, he should yield to her request for the preservation of his own. His servants joining their entreaties, Saul yielded at last, and the woman set before him the fatted calf and unleavened bread hastily prepared. What a scene!—In the wild cave of the sorceress, which but a little before had echoed with the words of doom—in the presence of Satan's messenger—he who had been anointed of God as king over Israel sat down to eat, in preparation for the day's deadly strife. Before the break of day he returned with his attendants to the camp of Israel to make ready for the conflict. By consulting that spirit of darkness Saul had destroyed himself. Oppressed by the horror of despair, it would be impossible for him to inspire his army with courage. Separated from the Source of strength, he could not lead the minds of Israel to look to God as their helper. Thus the prediction of evil would work its own accomplishment. On the plain of Shunem and the slopes of Mount Gilboa the armies of Israel and the hosts of the Philistines closed in mortal combat. Though the fearful scene in the cave of Endor had driven all hope from his heart, Saul fought with desperate valor for his throne and his kingdom. But it was in vain. "The men of Israel fled from before the Philistines, and fell down slain in Mount Gilboa." Three brave sons of the king died at his side. The archers pressed upon Saul. He had seen his soldiers falling around him and his princely sons cut down by the sword. Himself wounded, he could neither fight nor fly. Escape was impossible, and determined not to be taken alive by the Philistines, he bade his armor-bearer, "Draw thy sword, and thrust me through therewith." When the man refused to lift his hand against the Lord's anointed, Saul took his own life by falling upon his sword. Thus the first king of Israel perished, with the guilt of self-murder upon his soul. His life had been a failure, and he went down in dishonor and despair, because he had set up his own perverse will against the will of God. The tidings of defeat spread far and wide, carrying terror to all Israel. The people fled from the cities, and the Philistines took undisturbed possession. Saul's reign, independent of God, had well-nigh proved the ruin of his people. On the day following the engagement, the Philistines, searching the battlefield to rob the slain, discovered the bodies of Saul and his three sons. To complete their triumph, they cut off the head of Saul and stripped him of his armor; then the head and the armor, reeking with blood, were sent to the country of the Philistines as a trophy of victory, "to publish it in the house of their idols, and among the people." The armor was finally put in "the house of Ashtaroth," while the head was fastened in the temple of Dagon. Thus the glory of the victory was ascribed to the power of these false gods, and the name of Jehovah was dishonored. The dead bodies of Saul and his sons were dragged to Beth-shan, a city not far from Gilboa, and near the river Jordan. Here they were hung up in chains, to be devoured by birds of prey. But the brave men of Jabesh-gilead, remembering Saul's deliverance of their city in his earlier and happier years, now manifested their gratitude by rescuing the bodies of the king and princes, and giving them honorable burial. Crossing the Jordan by night, they "took the body of Saul and the bodies of his sons from the wall of Beth-shan, and came to Jabesh, and burnt them there, and they took their bones, and buried them under a tree at Jabesh, and fasted seven days." Thus the noble deed performed forty years before, secured for Saul and his sons burial by tender and pitying hands in that dark hour of defeat and dishonor.

MODERN SORCERY

—Ancient and Modern Sorcery The Scripture account of Saul's visit to the woman of Endor has been a source of perplexity to many students of the Bible. There are some who take the position that Samuel was actually present at the interview with Saul, but the Bible itself furnishes sufficient ground for a contrary conclusion. If, as claimed by some, Samuel was in heaven, he must have been summoned thence, either by the power of God or by that of Satan. None can believe for a moment that Satan had power to call the holy prophet of God from heaven to honor the incantations of an abandoned woman. Nor can we conclude that God summoned him to the witch's cave; for the Lord had already refused to communicate with Saul, by dreams, by Urim, or by prophets. 1 Samuel 28:6. These were God's own appointed mediums of communication, and He did not pass them by to deliver the message through the agent of Satan. The message itself is sufficient evidence of its origin. Its object was not to lead Saul to repentance, but to urge him on to ruin; and this is not the work of God, but of Satan. Furthermore, the act of Saul in consulting a sorceress is cited in Scripture as one reason why he was rejected by God and abandoned to destruction: "Saul died for his transgression which he committed against the Lord, even against the word of the Lord, which he kept not, and also for asking counsel of one that had a familiar spirit, to inquire of it; and inquired not of the Lord: therefore He slew him, and turned the kingdom unto David the son of Jesse." 1 Chronicles 10:13, 14. Here it is distinctly stated that Saul inquired of the familiar spirit, not of the Lord. He did not communicate with Samuel, the prophet of God; but through the sorceress he held intercourse with Satan. Satan could not present the real Samuel, but he did present a counterfeit, that served his purpose of deception. Nearly all forms of ancient sorcery and witchcraft were founded upon a belief in communion with the dead. Those who practiced the arts of necromancy claimed to have intercourse with departed spirits, and to obtain through them a knowledge of future events. This custom of consulting the dead is referred to in the prophecy of Isaiah: "When they shall say unto you, Seek unto them that have familiar spirits, and unto wizards that peep and that mutter: should not a people seek unto their God? for the living to the dead?" Isaiah 8:19. This same belief in communion with the dead formed the cornerstone of heathen idolatry. The gods of the heathen were believed to be the deified spirits of departed heroes. Thus the religion of the heathen was a worship of the dead. This is evident from the Scriptures. In the account of the sin of Israel at Beth-peor, it is stated: "Israel abode in Shittim, and the people began to commit whoredom with the daughters of Moab. And they called the people unto the sacrifices of their gods: and the people did eat, and bowed down to their gods. And Israel joined himself unto Baalpeor." Numbers 25:1-3. The psalmist tells us to what kind of gods these sacrifices were offered. Speaking of the same apostasy of the Israelites, he says, "They joined themselves also unto Baalpeor, and ate the sacrifices of the dead" (Psalm 106:28); that is, sacrifices that had been offered to the dead. The deification of the dead has held a prominent place in nearly every system of heathenism, as has also the supposed communion with the dead. The gods were believed to communicate their will to men, and also, when consulted, to give them counsel. Of this character were the famous oracles of Greece and Rome. The belief in communion with the dead is still held, even in professedly Christian lands. Under the name of spiritualism the practice of communicating with beings claiming to be the spirits of the departed has become widespread. It is calculated to take hold of the sympathies of those who have laid their loved ones in the grave. Spiritual beings sometimes appear to persons in the form of their deceased friends, and relate incidents connected with their lives and perform acts which they performed while living. In this way they lead men to believe that their dead friends are angels, hovering over them and communicating with them. Those who thus assume to be the spirits of the departed are regarded with a certain idolatry, and with many their word has greater weight than the word of God. There are many, however, who regard spiritualism as a mere imposture. The manifestations by which it supports its claims to a supernatural character are attributed to fraud on the part of the medium. But while it is true that the results of trickery have often been palmed off as genuine manifestations, there have also been marked evidences of supernatural power. And many who reject spiritualism as the result of human skill or cunning will, when confronted with manifestations which they cannot account for upon this ground, be led to acknowledge its claims. Modern spiritualism and the forms of ancient witchcraft and idol worship—all having communion with the dead as their vital principle—are founded upon that first lie by which Satan beguiled Eve in Eden: "Ye shall not surely die: for God doth know that in the day ye eat thereof, ... ye shall be as gods." Genesis 3:4, 5. Alike based upon falsehood and perpetuating the same, they are alike from the father of lies. The Hebrews were expressly forbidden to engage in any manner in pretended communion with the dead. God closed this door effectually when He said: "The dead know not anything.... Neither have they any more a portion forever in anything that is done under the sun." Ecclesiastes 9:5, 6. "His breath goeth forth, he returneth to his earth; in that very day his thoughts perish." Psalm 146:4. And the Lord declared to Israel: "The soul that turneth after such as have familiar spirits, and after wizards, to go a whoring after them, I will even set My face against that soul, and will cut him off from among his people." Leviticus 20:6. The "familiar spirits" were not the spirits of the dead, but evil angels, the messengers of Satan. Ancient idolatry, which, as we have seen, comprises both worship of the dead and pretended communion with them, is declared by the Bible to have been demon worship. The apostle Paul, in warning his brethren against participating, in any manner, in the idolatry of their heathen neighbors, says, "The things which the Gentiles sacrifice, they sacrifice to devils, and not to God, and I would not that ye should have fellowship with devils." 1 Corinthians 10:20. The psalmist, speaking of Israel, says that "they sacrificed their sons and their daughters unto devils," and in the next verse he explains that they sacrificed them "unto the idols of Canaan." Psalm 106:37, 38. In their supposed worship of dead men they were in reality worshiping demons. Modern spiritualism, resting upon the same foundation, is but a revival in a new form of the witchcraft and demon worship that God condemned and prohibited of old. It is foretold in the Scriptures, which declare that "in the latter times some shall depart from the faith, giving heed to seducing spirits, and doctrines of devils." 1 Timothy 4:1. Paul, in his second letter to the Thessalonians, points to the special working of Satan in spiritualism as an event to take place immediately before the second advent of Christ. Speaking of Christ's second coming, he declares that it is "after the working of Satan with all power and signs and lying wonders." 2 Thessalonians 2:9. And Peter, describing the dangers to which the church was to be exposed in the last days, says that as there were false prophets who led Israel into sin, so there will be false teachers, "who privily shall bring in damnable heresies, even denying the Lord that bought them.... And many shall follow their pernicious ways." 2 Peter 2:1, 2. Here the apostle has pointed out one of the marked characteristics of spiritualist teachers. They refuse to acknowledge Christ as the Son of God. Concerning such teachers the beloved John declares: "Who is a liar but he that denieth that Jesus is the Christ? He is antichrist, that denieth the Father and the Son. Whosoever denieth the Son, the same hath not the Father." 1 John 2:22, 23. Spiritualism, by denying Christ, denies both the Father and the Son, and the Bible pronounces it the manifestation of antichrist. By the prediction of Saul's doom, given through the woman of Endor, Satan planned to ensnare the people of Israel. He hoped that they would be inspired with confidence in the sorceress, and would be led to consult her. Thus they would turn from God as their counselor and would place themselves under the guidance of Satan. The lure by which spiritualism attracts the multitudes is its pretended power to draw aside the veil from the future and reveal to men what God has hidden. God has in His word opened before us the great events of the future—all that it is essential for us to know—and He has given us a safe guide for our feet amid all its perils; but it is Satan's purpose to destroy men's confidence in God, to make them dissatisfied with their condition in life, and to lead them to seek a knowledge of what God has wisely veiled from them, and to despise what He has revealed in

His Holy Word. There are many who become restless when they cannot know the definite outcome of affairs. They cannot endure uncertainty, and in their impatience they refuse to wait to see the salvation of God. Apprehended evils drive them nearly distracted. They give way to their rebellious feelings, and run hither and thither in passionate grief, seeking intelligence concerning that which has not been revealed. If they would but trust in God, and watch unto prayer, they would find divine consolation. Their spirit would be calmed by communion with God. The weary and the heavy-laden would find rest unto their souls if they would only go to Jesus; but when they neglect the means that God has ordained for their comfort, and resort to other sources, hoping to learn what God has withheld, they commit the error of Saul, and thereby gain only a knowledge of evil. God is not pleased with this course, and has expressed it in the most explicit terms. This impatient haste to tear away the veil from the future reveals a lack of faith in God and leaves the soul open to the suggestions of the master deceiver. Satan leads men to consult those that have familiar spirits; and by revealing hidden things of the past, he inspires confidence in his power to foretell things to come. By experience gained through the long ages he can reason from cause to effect and often forecast, with a degree of accuracy, some of the future events of man's life. Thus he is enabled to deceive poor, misguided souls and bring them under his power and lead them captive at his will. God has given us the warning by His prophet: "When they shall say unto you, Seek unto them that have familiar spirits, and unto wizards that peep and that mutter: should not a people seek unto their God? for the living to the dead? To the law and to the testimony: if they speak not according to this word, it is because there is no light in them." Isaiah 8:19, 20. Shall those who have a holy God, infinite in wisdom and power, go unto wizards, whose knowledge comes from intimacy with the enemy of our Lord? God Himself is the light of His people; He bids them fix their eyes by faith upon the glories that are veiled from human sight. The Sun of Righteousness sends its bright beams into their hearts; they have light from the throne of heaven, and they have no desire to turn away from the source of light to the messengers of Satan. The demon's message to Saul, although it was a denunciation of sin and a prophecy of retribution, was not meant to reform him, but to goad him to despair and ruin. Oftener, however, it serves the tempter's purpose best to lure men to destruction by flattery. The teaching of the demon gods in ancient times fostered the vilest license. The divine precepts condemning sin and enforcing righteousness were set aside; truth was lightly regarded, and impurity was not only permitted but enjoined. Spiritualism declares that there is no death, no sin, no judgment, no retribution; that "men are unfallen demigods;" that desire is the highest law; and that man is accountable only to himself. The barriers that God has erected to guard truth, purity, and reverence are broken down, and many are thus emboldened in sin. Does not such teaching suggest an origin similar to that of demon worship? The Lord presented before Israel the results of holding communion with evil spirits, in the abominations of the Canaanites: they were without natural affection, idolaters, adulterers, murderers, and abominable by every corrupt thought and revolting practice. Men do not know their own hearts; for "the heart is deceitful above all things, and desperately wicked." Jeremiah 17:9. But God understands the tendencies of the depraved nature of man. Then, as now, Satan was watching to bring about conditions favorable to rebellion, that the people of Israel might make themselves as abhorrent to God as were the Canaanites. The adversary of souls is ever on the alert to open channels for the unrestrained flow of evil in us; for he desires that we may be ruined, and be condemned before God. Satan was determined to keep his hold on the land of Canaan, and when it was made the habitation of the children of Israel, and the law of God was made the law of the land, he hated Israel with a cruel and malignant hatred and plotted their destruction. Through the agency of evil spirits strange gods were introduced; and because of transgression, the chosen people were finally scattered from the Land of Promise. This history Satan is striving to repeat in our day. God is leading His people out from the abominations of the world, that they may keep His law; and because of this, the rage of "the accuser of our brethren" knows no bounds. "The devil is come down unto you, having great wrath, because he knoweth that he hath but a short time." Revelation 12:10, 12. The antitypical land of promise is just before us, and Satan is determined to destroy the people of God and cut them off from their inheritance. The admonition, "Watch ye and pray, lest ye enter into temptation" (Mark 14:38), was never more needed than now. The word of the Lord to ancient Israel is addressed also to His people in this age: "Regard not them that have familiar spirits, neither seek after wizards, to be defiled by them;" "for all that do these things are an abomination unto the Lord." Leviticus 19:31; Deuteronomy 18:12.

SPIRITUALISM

The ministration of holy angels, as presented in the Scriptures, is a truth most comforting and precious to every follower of Christ. But the Bible teaching upon this point has been obscured and perverted by the errors of popular theology. The doctrine of natural immortality, first borrowed from the pagan philosophy, and in the darkness of the great apostasy incorporated into the Christian faith, has supplanted the truth, so plainly taught in Scripture, that "the dead know not anything." Multitudes have come to believe that it is the spirits of the dead who are the "ministering spirits sent forth to minister for them who shall be heirs of salvation." And this notwithstanding the testimony of Scripture to the existence of heavenly angels, and their connection with the history of man, before the death of a human being. The doctrine of man's consciousness in death, especially the belief that the spirits of the dead return to minister to the living, has prepared the way for modern Spiritualism. If the dead are admitted to the presence of God and holy angels, and privileged with knowledge far exceeding what they before possessed, why should they not return to the earth to enlighten and instruct the living? If, as taught by popular theologians, the spirits of the dead are hovering about their friends on earth, why should they not be permitted to communicate with them, to warn them against evil, or to comfort them in sorrow? How can those who believe in man's consciousness in death reject what comes to them as divine light communicated by glorified spirits? Here is a channel regarded as sacred, through which Satan works for the accomplishment of his purposes. The fallen angels who do his bidding appear as messengers from the spirit world. While professing to bring the living into communication with the dead, the prince of evil exercises his bewitching influence upon their minds. He has power to bring before men the appearance of their departed friends. The counterfeit is perfect; the familiar look, the words, the tone, are reproduced with marvelous distinctness. Many are comforted with the assurance that their loved ones are enjoying the bliss of Heaven; and without suspicion of danger, they give ear to “seducing spirits, and doctrines of devils.” When they have been led to believe that the dead actually return to communicate with them, Satan causes those to appear who went into the grave unprepared. They claim to be happy in Heaven, and even to occupy exalted positions there; and thus the error is widely taught, that no difference is made between the righteous and the wicked. The pretended visitants from the world of spirits sometimes utter cautions and warnings which prove to be correct. Then, as confidence is gained, they present doctrines that directly undermine faith in the Scriptures. With an appearance of deep interest in the well-being of their friends on earth, they insinuate the most dangerous errors. The fact that they state some truths, and are able at times to foretell future events, gives to their statements an appearance of reliability; and their false teachings are accepted by the multitudes as readily, and believed as implicitly, as if they were the most sacred truths of the Bible. The law of God is set aside, the Spirit of grace despised, the blood of the covenant counted an unholy thing. The spirits deny the divinity of Christ, and place even the Creator on a level with themselves. Thus under a new disguise the great rebel still carries forward his warfare against God, begun in Heaven, and for nearly six thousand years continued upon the earth. Many endeavor to account for spiritual manifestations by attributing them wholly to fraud and sleight of hand on the part of the medium. But while it is true that the results of trickery have often been palmed off as genuine manifestations, there have been, also, marked exhibitions of supernatural power. The mysterious rapping with which modern Spiritualism began was not the result of human trickery or cunning, but was the direct work of evil angels, who thus introduced one of the most successful of soul-destroying delusions. Many will be ensnared through the belief that Spiritualism is a merely human imposture; when brought face to face with manifestations which they cannot but regard as supernatural, they will be deceived, and will be led to accept them as the great power of God. These persons overlook the testimony of the Scriptures concerning the wonders wrought by Satan and his agents. It was by Satanic aid that Pharaoh's magicians were enabled to counterfeit the work of God. Paul testifies that before the second advent of Christ there will be similar manifestations of Satanic power. The coming of the Lord is to be preceded by "the working of Satan with all power and signs and lying wonders, and with all deceivableness of unrighteousness." [2 Thessalonians 2:9, 10.] And the apostle John, describing the miracle-working power that will be manifested in the last days, declares: "He doeth great wonders, so that he maketh fire come down from heaven on the earth in the sight of men, and deceiveth them that dwell on the earth by the means of those miracles which he had power to do." [Revelation 13:13, 14.] No mere impostures are here foretold. Men are deceived by the miracles which Satan's agents have power to do, not which they pretend to do. The prince of darkness, who has so long bent the powers of his master-mind to the work of deception, skillfully adapts his temptations to men of all classes and conditions. To persons of culture and refinement he presents Spiritualism in its more refined and intellectual aspects, and thus succeeds in drawing many into his snare. The wisdom which Spiritualism imparts is that described by the apostle James, which "descendeth not from above, but is earthly, sensual, devilish." [James 3:15.] This, however, the great deceiver conceals, when concealment will best suit his purpose. He who could appear clothed with the brightness of the heavenly seraphs before Christ in the wilderness of temptation, comes to men in the most attractive manner, as an angel of light. He appeals to the reason by the presentation of elevating themes, he delights the fancy with enrapturing scenes, and he enlists the affections by his eloquent portrayals of love and charity. He excites the imagination to lofty flights, leading men to take so great pride in their own wisdom that in their hearts they despise the Eternal One. That mighty being who could take the world's Redeemer to an exceedingly high mountain, and bring before him all the kingdoms of the earth and the glory of them, will present his temptations to men in a manner to pervert the senses of all who are not shielded by divine power. Satan beguiles men now as he beguiled Eve in Eden, by flattery, by kindling a desire to obtain forbidden knowledge, by exciting ambition for self-exaltation. It was cherishing these evils that caused his fall, and through them he aims to compass the ruin of men. "Ye shall be as gods," he declares, "knowing good and evil." [Genesis 3:5.] Spiritualism teaches "that man is the creature of progression; that it is his destiny from his birth to progress, even to eternity, toward the Godhead," And again: "Each mind will judge itself and not another." "The judgment will be right, because it is the judgment of self.... The throne is within you." Said a Spiritualistic teacher, as the "spiritual consciousness" awoke within him, "My fellow-men, all were unfallen demigods." And another declares, "Any just and perfect being is Christ. Thus, in place of the righteousness and perfection of the infinite God, the true object of adoration; in place of the perfect righteousness of his law, the true standard of human attainment, Satan has substituted the sinful, erring nature of man himself, as the only object of adoration, the only rule of judgment, or standard of character. This is progress, not upward, but downward. It is a law both of the intellectual and the spiritual nature, that by beholding, we become changed. The mind gradually adapts itself to the subjects upon which it is allowed to dwell. It becomes assimilated to that which it is accustomed to love and reverence. Man will never rise higher than his standard of purity or goodness or truth. If self is his loftiest ideal, he will never attain to anything more exalted. Rather, he will constantly sink lower and lower. The grace of God alone has power to exalt man. Left to himself, his course must inevitably be downward. To the self-indulgent, the pleasure-loving, the sensual, Spiritualism presents itself under a less subtle disguise than to the more refined and intellectual; in its grosser forms they find that which is in harmony with their inclinations. Satan studies every indication of the frailty of human nature, he marks the sins which each individual is inclined to commit, and then he takes care that opportunities shall not be wanting to gratify the tendency to evil. He tempts men to excess in that which is in itself lawful, causing them, through intemperance, to weaken physical, mental, and moral power. He has destroyed and is destroying thousands through the indulgence of the passions, thus brutalizing the entire nature of man. And to complete his work, he declares, through the spirits, that "true knowledge places man above all law;" that "whatsoever is, is right;" that "God doth not condemn;" and that "all sins which are committed are innocent." When the people are thus led to believe that desire is the highest law, that liberty is license, and that man is accountable only to himself, who can wonder that corruption and depravity teem on every hand? Multitudes eagerly accept teachings that leave them at liberty to obey the promptings of the carnal heart. The reins of self-control are laid upon the neck of lust, the powers of mind and soul are made subject to the animal propensities, and Satan exultingly sweeps into his net thousands who profess to be followers of Christ. But none need be deceived by the lying claims of Spiritualism. God has given the world sufficient light to enable them to discover the snare. As already shown, the theory which forms the very foundation of Spiritualism is at war with the plainest statements of Scripture. The Bible declares that the dead know not anything, that their thoughts have perished; they have no part in anything that is done under the sun; they know nothing of the joys or sorrows of those who were dearest to them on earth. Furthermore, God has expressly forbidden all pretended communication with departed spirits. In the days of the Hebrews there was a class of people who claimed, as do the Spiritualists of today, to hold communication with the dead. But the "familiar spirits," as these visitants from other worlds were called, are declared by the Bible to be the "spirits of devils." [Compare Numbers 25:1-3; Psalm 106:28; 1 Corinthians 10:20; Revelation 16:14.] The work of dealing with familiar spirits was pronounced an abomination to the Lord, and was solemnly forbidden under penalty of death. [Leviticus 19:31; 20:27.] The very name of witchcraft is now held in contempt. The claim that men can hold intercourse with evil spirits is regarded as a fable of the Dark Ages. But Spiritualism, which numbers its converts by hundreds of thousands, yea, by millions, which has made its way into scientific circles, which has invaded churches, and has found favor in legislative bodies, and even in the courts of kings—this mammoth deception is but a revival, in a new disguise, of the witchcraft condemned and prohibited of old. If there were no other evidence of the real character of Spiritualism, it should be enough for the Christian that the spirits make no difference between righteousness and sin, between the noblest and purest of the apostles of Christ and the most corrupt of the servants of Satan. By representing the basest of men as in Heaven, and highly exalted there, Satan says to the world: "No matter how wicked you are; no matter whether you believe or disbelieve God and the Bible. Live as you please; Heaven is your home." The Spiritualist teachers virtually declare, "Every one that doeth evil is good in the sight of the Lord, and he delighteth in them; or, Where is the God of judgment?" [Malachi 2:17.] Saith the Word of God, "Woe unto them that call evil good, and good evil; that put darkness for light, and light for darkness." [Isaiah 5:20.] The apostles, as personated by these lying spirits, are made to contradict what they wrote at the dictation of the Holy Spirit when on earth. They deny the divine origin of the Bible, and thus tear away the foundation of the Christian's hope, and put out the light that reveals the way to Heaven. Satan is making the world believe that the Bible is a mere fiction, or at least a book suited to the infancy of the race, but now to be lightly regarded, or cast aside as obsolete. And to take the place of the Word of God he holds out spiritual manifestations. Here is a channel wholly under his control; by this means he can make the world believe what he will. The Book that is to judge him and his followers he puts in the shade, just where he wants it; the Saviour of the world he makes to be no more than a common man. And as the Roman guard that watched the tomb of Jesus spread the lying report which the priests and elders put into their mouths to disprove his resurrection, so do the believers in spiritual manifestations try to make it appear that there is nothing miraculous in the circumstances of our Saviour's life. After thus seeking to put Jesus in the background, they call attention to their own miracles, declaring that these far exceed the works of Christ. It is true that Spiritualism is now changing its form, and, veiling some of its more objectionable features, is assuming a Christian guise. But its utterances from the platform and the press have been before the public for nearly forty years, and in these its real character stands revealed. These teachings cannot be denied or hidden.

Even in its present form, so far from being more worthy of toleration than formerly, it is really a more dangerous, because a more subtle deception. While it formerly denounced Christ and the Bible, it now professes to accept both. But the Bible is interpreted in a manner that is pleasing to the unrenewed heart, while its solemn and vital truths are made of no effect. Love is dwelt upon as the chief attribute of God, but it is degraded to a weak sentimentalism making little distinction between good and evil. God's justice, his denunciations of sin, the requirements of his holy law, are all kept out of sight. The people are taught to regard the decalogue as a dead letter. Pleasing, bewitching fables captivate the senses, and lead men to reject the Bible as the foundation of their faith. Christ is as verily denied as before; but Satan has so blinded the eyes of the people that the deception is not discerned. There are few who have any just conception of the deceptive power of Spiritualism and the danger of coming under its influence. Many tamper with it, merely to gratify their curiosity. They have no real faith in it, and would be filled with horror at the thought of yielding themselves to the spirits' control. But they venture upon the forbidden ground, and the mighty destroyer exercises his power upon them against their will. Let them once be induced to submit their minds to his direction, and he holds them captive. It is impossible, in their own strength, to break away from the bewitching, alluring spell. Nothing but the power of God, granted in answer to the earnest prayer of faith, can deliver these ensnared souls. All who indulge sinful traits of character, or willfully cherish a known sin, are inviting the temptations of Satan. They separate themselves from God and from the watchcare of his angels; as the evil one presents his deceptions, they are without defense, and fall an easy prey. Those who thus place themselves in his power, little realize where their course will end. Having achieved their overthrow, the tempter will employ them as his agents to lure others to ruin. Says the prophet Isaiah: "When they shall say unto you, Seek unto them that have familiar spirits, and unto wizards that peep, and that mutter: should not a people seek unto their God? for the living to the dead? To the law and to the testimony. If they speak not according to this word, it is because there is no light in them." [Isaiah 8:19, 20.] If men had been willing to receive the truth so plainly stated in the Scriptures, concerning the nature of man and the state of the dead, they would see in the claims and manifestations of Spiritualism the working of Satan with power and signs and lying wonders. But rather than yield the liberty so agreeable to the carnal heart, and renounce the sins which they love, multitudes close their eyes to the light, and walk straight on, regardless of warnings, while Satan weaves his snares about them, and they become his prey. “Because they received not the love of the truth, that they might be saved,” therefore “God shall send them strong delusion, that they should believe a lie.” [2 Thessalonians 2:10, 11.] Those who oppose the teachings of Spiritualism are assailing, not men alone, but Satan and his angels. They have entered upon a contest against principalities and powers and wicked spirits in high places. Satan will not yield one inch of ground except as he is driven back by the power of heavenly messengers. The people of God should be able to meet him, as did our Saviour, with the words, “It is written.” Satan can quote Scripture now as in the days of Christ, and he will pervert its teachings to sustain his delusions. Those who would stand in this time of peril must understand for themselves the testimony of the Scriptures. Many will be confronted by the spirits of devils personating beloved relatives or friends, and declaring the most dangerous heresies. These visitants will appeal to our tenderest sympathies, and will work miracles to sustain their pretensions. We must be prepared to withstand them with the Bible truth that the dead know not anything, and that they who thus appear are the spirits of devils. Just before us is the “hour of temptation, which shall come upon all the world, to try them that dwell upon the earth.”

[Revelation 3:10.] All whose faith is not firmly established upon the Word of God will be deceived and overcome. Satan "works with all deceivableness of unrighteousness" to gain control of the children of men; and his deceptions will continually increase. But he can gain his object only as men voluntarily yield to his temptations. Those who are earnestly seeking a knowledge of the truth, and are striving to purify their souls through obedience, thus doing what they can to prepare for the conflict, will find, in the God of truth, a sure defense. "Because thou hast kept the word of my patience, I also will keep thee," [Revelation 3:10.] is the Saviour's promise. He would sooner send every angel out of Heaven to protect his people, than leave one soul that trusts in him to be overcome by Satan. The prophet Isaiah brings to view the fearful deception which will come upon the wicked, causing them to count themselves secure from the judgments of God: "We have made a covenant with death, and with hell are we at agreement; when the overflowing scourge shall pass through, it shall not come unto us; for we have made lies our refuge, and under the falsehood have we hid ourselves." [Isaiah 28:15.] In the class here described are included those who in their stubborn impenitence comfort themselves with the assurance that there is to be no punishment for the sinner; that all mankind, it matters not how corrupt, are to be exalted to Heaven, to become as the angels of God. But still more emphatically are those making a covenant with death and an agreement with hell, who renounce the truths which Heaven has provided as a defense for the righteous in the day of trouble, and accept the refuge of lies offered by Satan in its stead,—the delusive pretensions of Spiritualism. Marvelous beyond expression is the blindness of the people of this generation. Thousands reject the Word of God as unworthy of belief, and with eager confidence receive the deceptions of Satan. Skeptics and scoffers denounce the bigotry of those who contend for the faith of prophets and apostles, and they divert themselves by holding up to ridicule the solemn declarations of the Scriptures concerning Christ and the plan of salvation, and the retribution to be visited upon the rejecters of the truth. They affect great pity for minds so narrow, weak, and superstitious as to acknowledge the claims of God, and obey the requirements of his law. They manifest as much assurance as if, indeed, they had made a covenant with death and an agreement with hell,—as if they had erected an impassable, impenetrable barrier between themselves and the vengeance of God. Nothing can arouse their fears. So fully have they yielded to the tempter, so closely are they united with him, and so thoroughly imbued with his spirit, that they have no power and no inclination to break away from his snare. Satan has long been preparing for his final effort to deceive the world. The foundation of his work was laid by the assurance given to Eve in Eden, "Ye shall not surely die." "In the day ye eat thereof, then your eyes shall be opened, and ye shall be as gods, knowing good and evil." [Genesis 3:4, 5.] Little by little he has prepared the way for his master-piece of deception in the development of Spiritualism. He has not yet reached the full accomplishment of his designs; but it will be reached in the last remnant of time. Says the prophet: "I saw three unclean spirits like frogs; ... they are the spirits of devils, working miracles, which go forth unto the kings of the earth and of the whole world, to gather them to the battle of that great day of God Almighty." [Revelation 16:13, 14.] Except those who are kept by the power of God, through faith in his Word, the whole world will be swept into the ranks of this delusion. The people are fast being lulled to a fatal security, to be awakened only by the outpouring of the wrath of God. Saith the Lord God: "Judgment also will I lay to the line, and righteousness to the plummet; and the hail shall sweep away the refuge of lies, and the waters shall overflow the hiding-place. And your covenant with death shall be disannulled, and your agreement with hell shall not stand; when the overflowing scourge shall pass through, then ye shall be trodden down by it." [Isaiah 28:17, 18.]

Made in the USA
Las Vegas, NV
17 May 2024

90038548R00022